Us

How to draw
Princesses
and
Ballerinas

Fiona Watt

Designed and illustrated by
Antonia Miller, Jan McCafferty, Non Figg,
Katie Lovell and Stella Baggott

Photographs by Howard Allman

Contents

Little Princesses

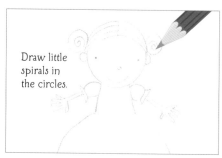

Draw little spirals in the circles.

Draw over the lines when the paint has dried.

1. Draw a circle for a head. Add her face and ears. Then, draw the bodice and skirt of her dress. Add little shapes for the toes of her shoes.

2. For her hair, draw lines on her head, then add a circle above each ear. Draw puffed sleeves, then add her arms and hands.

3. Draw a crown, then add patterns and lace to her dress. Fill her in with watery paints. Then, go over the lines with a black felt-tip pen.

Use the ideas shown in this picture to draw princesses doing different things.

4. To do a princess peeking out from behind a bush, draw the head and dress leaning over slightly. Add her arms at an angle, too.

5. Draw a bush overlapping the princess's skirt and arm. Then, erase the parts of the skirt and arm that are inside the bush.

6. Draw lots of circles for roses on the bush. Then, draw a spiral in each one. Paint your drawing, then go over the outlines with a pen.

If you want to draw a pond, like this, do the outline first, then draw the grass, fish and boat before you fill it in.

You could draw a princess picking flowers.

There are different styles of crowns and tiaras on page 32.

Princesses in pretty dresses

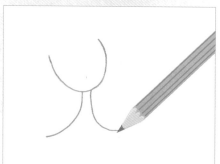

1. Use a pencil to draw a *U* shape for the face, drawing it near to the top of your paper. Then, add two long curves for her neck.

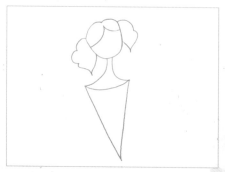

2. Draw two lines at the top of her face for the parting in her hair. Then, do the rest of her hair. Draw a V shape for her bodice, and a curved neckline.

You could draw your princess carrying a bag, a fan or even a little dog.

Start her skirt here.

3. Starting just above the point of the bodice, draw the outline of her skirt, like this. Then, draw two curved lines on the skirt.

4. Draw two ovals for the top part of her sleeves. Then, add the bottom part, giving it a frilly edge. Draw small shapes for her hands, too.

Draw thin lines inside her skirt, too.

5. Draw over all your pencil lines with felt-tip pens. Draw thicker bands around her neckline, sleeves, waist and skirt. Then, fill in her hair.

The dress above had pink
and orange pencil lines
added to the yellow part
of the skirt.

Don't brush
over the
thick bands.

You could
draw ribbons
in her hair.

6. Dip a paintbrush into some
water, then brush carefully
over the pen lines so that the
ink runs. Brush the watery
ink so that it fills the shape.

7. When the ink is dry, draw
her eyes with a black felt-tip
pen. *Use pencils to draw her
nose, lips and cheeks. Add
a crown with a gold pen.*

8. *Use pencils to draw over
all the outlines again. Then,
decorate her dress with bows
and frilly lace. Add patterns
with a gold pen, too.*

Princess castle

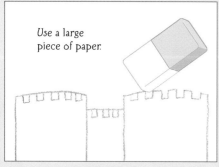

1. Draw two towers at the bottom of your paper, then add a line joining them. Draw squares along the tops, then erase the top of each square.

2. Draw two smaller towers on top, like this. Add a pointed roof on one of them, and add a roof and another turret on the other one.

3. Draw a sloping roof in the middle. Then, add more towers and turrets. Draw lots of pointed windows, and bricks on the walls.

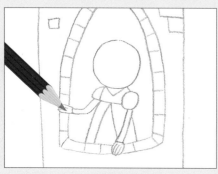

4. Draw a head in one of the windows and add the body. Then, draw one arm touching the window sill and the other out to one side.

5. Draw in her face. Then, add curved and wavy lines for her hair. Draw a little crown on top of her head, then add a little bird in her hand.

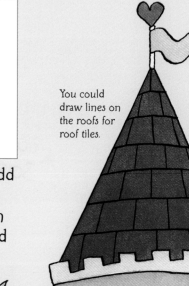

You could draw lines on the roofs for roof tiles.

6. Erase the lines where the bird, her arm and her hair overlap the window. Fill in your picture with paint, then go over the lines with a pen.

Draw a princess in every window.

You could draw a bird on some of the window sills.

Draw flags or hearts on top of each turret.

You could draw roses growing up the castle walls.

7

A family photograph

1. Draw a skirt on a piece of pink or shiny paper and cut it out. Cut a rectangle for the body, then glue both shapes onto a piece of white paper.

2. Cut out circles for the puffs on the sleeves and glue them on. Add the bottom part of the sleeves. Glue thin strips of paper across the skirt.

3. Use paint or felt-tip pens to draw a head and neck. Then, add her hair. Draw hands on a separate piece of paper, cut them out and glue them on.

All the people in this picture were made separately, then cut out and arranged on a long piece of paper.

You could add bodyguards standing on either side of the king.

Grown-up princesses

A royal dog

A little prince

4. Draw a little dot for each eye. Then, add a curved line for an eyelid. Draw her nose, lips and cheeks with a red pencil. Add a shiny crown.

5. For a little prince, cut out his clothes, hands and legs, and glue them down. Cut out shoes, a sash and circles for the tops of his sleeves.

6. Use paint or felt-tip pens to draw his head and neck. Then, add his hair. Draw his eyes, nose and mouth. Glue on a shiny crown.

You could use a gold pen to draw patterns on the background.

A grumpy royal uncle

The King

A little princess

This red carpet was glued down before all the people were added.

Another little prince

9

Dancing princesses

Use the ideas here to draw princesses dancing in different positions.

Start drawing near the top of the paper.

1. Use a pencil to draw a rectangle for the bodice of the princess' dress. Add two lines for her neck above it, then draw her head.

2. Draw two curved lines for the parting in her hair, then add little curly lines at the ends of them. Draw lots of long wavy hair, too.

3. Draw a little crown on top of her head. Then, add two shapes on either side of her neck, for a collar. Draw her eyes, nose and lips.

4. Draw one sleeve coming out to one side, then draw the other one coming in front of her bodice. Then, draw both her hands.

You could decorate the paper around your princesses with little dots of paint.

If you want to paint shadows under your dancing princesses, use very watery paint.

Add long ribbons coming from the bow.

Paint the bow in the same shade as her sash.

5. Draw the skirt of her dress with a curved bottom edge. Draw her shoes, too. Then, add a sash around her waist and a bow at the side.

6. Fill in her dress with watery paint. Mix paint for her skin, then paint her face, neck and hands. Paint her hair, shoes and sash, too.

7. Decorate her dress, sash and bow with hearts and dots. When the paint is dry, draw over all the pencil lines with a thin black felt-tip pen.

A princess sleepover

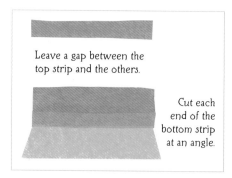

Leave a gap between the top strip and the others.

Cut each end of the bottom strip at an angle.

1. Cut a strip of tissue paper for the bottom of the bed and glue it in the middle of your paper. Cut three more strips and glue them on above.

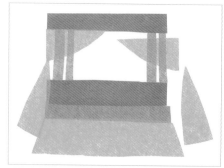

2. Cut four thin strips of paper for the posts on the bed and glue them on. Then, cut shapes for the curtains and glue them on top.

3. Draw lines around the curtains, posts and layers of the bed. Then, draw hearts, dots and other pretty patterns with a gold pen.

4. For a princess, cut a curved shape from tissue paper as the bottom layer of her skirt. Glue it on then cut two more shapes and glue them on top.

Make the bodice overlap the skirt a little.

5. Cut a rectangle for the bodice of the dress and glue it on. Add two long triangles for sleeves, then cut out circles and glue them on top.

6. *Use a thin black felt-tip pen to draw two short lines for her neck. Add a curve for her face, then draw lots of wavy lines for her hair.*

7. Draw around the top layer of the skirt, then draw along the sides and bottom of the other two layers. Add hands, and frills on her sleeves.

8. Draw eyes and a mouth. Use a red pencil to draw a line for her nose, and her cheeks. Then, fill in her hair with a yellow pencil.

9. Draw a crown with a gold pen. Then, decorate her skirt, sleeves and body with patterns drawn with black and gold pens.

A princess sleeps here

Decorate the bedroom walls with hearts and pictures.

You could glue tissue paper tassels on the curtains.

Add some slippers next to the bed.

If you glue a princess overlapping the bed, fill in her face with a dark pencil, so that the tissue paper doesn't show through.

A princess and a frog prince

You could draw some butterflies and dragonflies around the princess.

These clouds were drawn with white wax crayon, then the sky was painted over them.

Draw grasses and reeds around the pond.

To do a big scene like this, draw the princess and the frog, then add the pond.

1. *Use a pencil to draw two green ovals for the skirt. Then, draw a purple curve between them. Add a bodice, sleeves and the shoes.*

2. Draw the neck, face and hair with an ordinary pencil. Then, use different pencils to draw her arms, a crown and a flower in her hands.

3. Use pink, green and orange wax crayons to draw patterns on the princess' dress. Then, draw pink lines in her hair and add circles on her cheeks.

Paint inside the crayon lines.

4. Mix some watery purple paint and use it to fill in her bodice, sleeves and parts of her skirt. Fill in the rest with other shades of watery paint.

5. Paint her face, arms, shoes and the crown. Then, paint her hair. When the paint is dry, draw over her eyes, nose, mouth and skirt again.

Use different shades of green crayons.

6. Draw the outline of a frog, then add eyes, a mouth and a crown. Draw green spots and pink cheeks with wax crayons, then add a lily pad.

7. Paint the frog and lily pad with different shades of watery paint. When the paint is dry, draw over your pencil and crayon lines again.

A royal carriage

Draw a princess looking out of the window (see pages 6-7 and page 32 for ideas).

You could draw striped curtains in the windows.

Use a thin felt-tip pen.

1. Draw rectangles for the roof and the main part of the carriage. Add a wheel at each bottom corner, then draw the part between them.

2. Draw three windows, then add double lines separating them. Draw spokes on the wheels, then add a curved bar at the bottom.

Draw a crown on the roof.

3. Draw a curly S shape above each wheel. Then, decorate the carriage with lots of flowers and patterns. Fill in the coach with pencils.

Princess bride

Decorate the top of her dress with flowers, too.

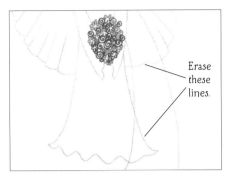

Erase these lines.

1. Draw a head, neck, eyes and nose with a brown pencil. Then, add pink shoulders. Draw her wavy hair, tiara and lips with felt-tip pens.

2. Use a pink pencil to draw a dress, with a wavy bottom. Draw swirls and hearts for her bouquet with red and pink pens. Then, draw the sleeves.

3. Draw a long train and veil with a pink pencil. Then, erase the pencil lines where the train overlaps the veil and the dress.

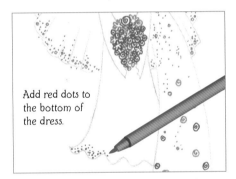

Add red dots to the bottom of the dress.

4. Add lots of red and pink felt-tip pen dots and circles to the edge of her veil. Draw dots, circles and spirals on her train and dress, too.

For confetti, draw hearts and spirals with felt-tip pens and dab them with water.

You could draw steps behind the princess' dress and shade them with a pencil.

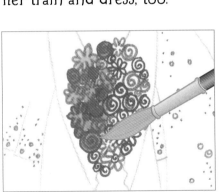

5. Dip a paintbrush into clean water and dab it over her hair and bouquet to make the ink run. Do the same with all the dots and spirals.

Sweet ballerinas

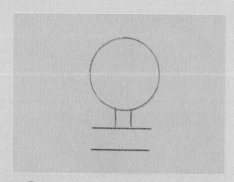

Use yellow and white chalks.

Paint across her shoulders, too.

1. Draw a circle for the head at the top of a piece of bright paper. Add two short lines for her neck. Then, draw two lines for her shoulders.

2. Use a chalk pastel or a piece of chalk to draw the bodice of her skirt. Then, draw lots of long zigzagging lines beneath it for the skirt.

3. Mix some paint for her skin using shades of red, yellow, white and a tiny amount of blue paint. Fill in her face and neck. Then, paint her arms.

These ballerinas show you some different positions for your ballerina's arms, legs and feet.

For a darker skin tone, add a little blue paint to a mixture of red, yellow and white.

18

You could decorate the
paper around your ballerina
with little butterflies.

4. Paint legs coming from
beneath her skirt. Then, add
the feet. If your ballerina is
pointing her toes, then paint
a straight leg, with no foot.

5. When the paint has dried,
use chalk to draw her hair.
Add ribbons in her hair and
on her shoulders. Then, draw
her face with pens or pencils.

6. Use the chalk to draw her
ballet shoes. Add crossed
lines around her ankles and
add tiny bows. Then, draw
a ribbon around her waist.

Ballerinas at the barre

Use watery paint to paint reflections on the mirror.

A barre is a rail that dancers hold onto in a ballet class to help them balance.

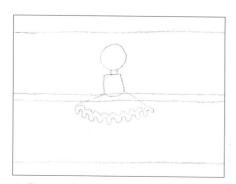

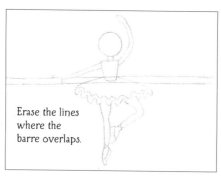

Erase the lines where the barre overlaps.

1. Draw a rectangle for a mirror and two lines across the middle of your paper for the barre. Draw the ballerina's head, neck and tutu.

2. Draw one arm holding onto the barre and the other one curving above the head. Draw one straight leg and the other one bent at the knee.

3. Draw the hair on her head. Draw loops for a tiara across the top of her head, then add a bun on top. Draw her face and ringlets, too.

Draw little curved lines to show that the ballerina's arms are moving.

Fill in between the wavy lines of the tutus with a darker shade of paint.

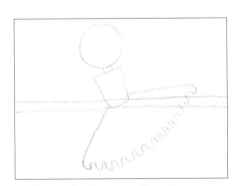

4. For a ballerina dancing sideways, draw the bodice of her tutu overlapping the barre. Then, add the skirt and her head and neck.

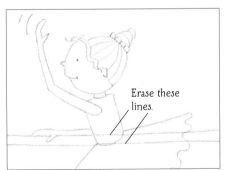

Erase these lines.

5. Draw one arm along the top of the barre and the other one curving in front. Add her hair. Erase all the lines where the barre overlaps.

Use pens to draw over the lines.

6. Draw the legs, a sash and ballet shoes. Then, paint all the ballerinas with watery paints. When the paint is dry, draw over the lines.

Swan Lake

You could decorate your drawing with little swans on the lake.

In the ballet, Swan Lake, a beautiful girl is changed into a swan by a wicked magician.

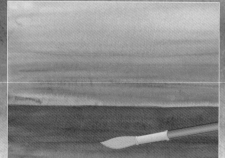

1. Brush blue watery paint all over a piece of paper and leave it to dry a little. Then, paint more blue paint across the bottom half for a lake.

2. Draw the moon with white chalk or a chalk pastel. Then, go around it in yellow. Add white and yellow lines on the lake for the reflection.

3. Draw a white curved shape for the ballerina's bodice. Then, draw lots of slightly curved lines coming from it for her skirt.

Lots of ballerinas in Swan Lake dance dressed as swans.

4. *Use a pale chalk or chalk pastel to draw lines for her arms, legs and neck. Draw her head, then add a white tiara and ballet shoes.*

5. Brush a fingertip along the lines on the skirt to smudge the chalk. Then, smudge the bodice, arms, legs, head and the moon, a little, too.

6. Draw some little lines for sleeves at the tops of her arms. Then, decorate her skirt, crown and around her neck with glitter glue.

Sugar Plum Fairy

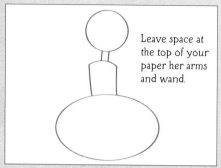

1. Draw a head and add a neck and a bodice on a piece of thick white paper. Then, draw an oval for the bottom layer of the ballerina's skirt.

2. Draw the ballerina's arms. Then, draw her legs, overlapping the skirt a little. Draw her face and hair, then her wings and a wand.

3. Mix some watery pink paint and brush it all over the ballerina. The pencil lines should still show through the paint. Then, leave it to dry.

4. Mix thick paint for her skin and fill in her face, arms and the top of her body. *Use other thick paints to fill in her eyes, legs, hair and wings.*

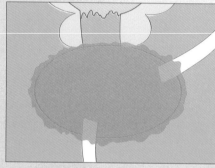

5. Rip an oval of pink or purple tissue paper about the size of the skirt. Glue it onto the paper so that it overlaps the tops of the legs.

6. Cut a strip of pink tissue paper for the top layer of the skirt. Gather it along one edge, then glue this edge along the ballerina's waist.

7. Cut a small bodice from pink paper. Cut a V shape in the top, then glue the bodice on so that it overlaps the gathered edge of the skirt.

8. Draw over her lips, nose, eyelashes and cheeks with pencils. *Use pens to draw her ballet shoes and for the ribbons around her legs.*

9. Brush glue onto her wand and in a band across her waist. Sprinkle it with glitter. Shake off any extra glitter when the glue is dry.

The Sugar Plum Fairy appears in a ballet called The Nutcracker. She lives in the Land of Sweets.

You could cut around your Sugar Plum Fairy and glue her onto a painted stage.

Decorate the stage with pictures of sweets.

Leaping ballerinas

Draw a rough spiral for the hair on top of her head.

1. *Use a thin black felt-tip pen to draw an oval for a head. Draw it about a third of the way from the top of your paper. Then, add the hair.*

You could draw your ballerina on pale pink or lilac paper instead of white paper.

Use the ideas shown here to draw other leaping ballerinas.

2. Draw curved lines for her neck. Then, join the lines with a *U* shape for the neckline of her tutu. Draw two more curved lines for her body.

3. *Use a pink felt-tip pen to draw a circle with a spiral inside for each sleeve. Then, draw looping lines below her body for her tutu.*

4. Dip a clean paintbrush into some water, then gently brush it over all the felt-tip pen lines so that the ink runs. Leave it to dry.

Start here.

5. Starting at the edge of her tutu, draw a bent leg with a pointed foot. Add the other leg coming out at the same angle. Draw ballet shoes.

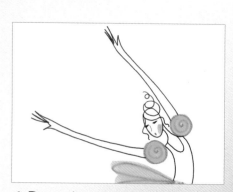

6. Draw long arms with stretched-out fingers. Then, use a pen to draw her eyes, and add a nose, mouth and cheeks with a pink pencil.

Use a pencil to fill in her hair, too.

7. Fill in the bodice of her tutu and her ballet shoes with a pink pencil. Add a band at the edge of each sleeve and draw ribbons around her legs.

You could draw hearts around your ballerina.

In the ballet, The Firebird, the Firebird gives a prince a magic feather, which he can use to call her when he is in danger.

You could paint lots of patterned feathers around your ballerina.

28

Firebird ballerina

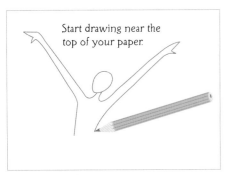

Start drawing near the top of your paper.

1. Draw an oval for the ballerina's head, then add two curved lines for her neck. Draw her arms stretching up and add her body.

2. For her skirt, draw a line below her body. Then, draw a half circle from one end of the line to the other. Add her legs and feet.

Leave a paler area around the ballerina.

3. Mix watery yellow and pink paint. Then, paint water all over the paper to dampen it. Brush the paints over the wet paper so that they run.

Use pens to draw her face.

4. When the paint has dried, mix some paint for her skin. Fill in her face, neck, arms and legs. Paint some shoes, too. Then, draw her face.

Glue the pointed end of the feathers.

5. Cut several "feathers" from pink crêpe paper or tissue paper. Spread glue halfway along each one and press them onto the skirt.

Make the feathers come up over the outline of the skirt.

6. Add another layer of pink feathers, then a layer of orange ones. Glue pointed feathers on top. Then, cut feathers from shiny paper and glue them on.

Use pink paper for the bodice.

7. Draw a curved shape with a point at the bottom, for the bodice. Cut it out and glue it on, so that it covers the ends of the feathers.

The crescent shape should fit the head.

8. For the headdress, cut out pointed feathers. Glue them on in a fan shape. Then, cut a crescent shape and glue it over the ends of the feathers.

9. Decorate the dress and headdress with paint and a gold pen. Then, to make the feathers curl, carefully roll each one around a pencil.

Ballerina paperchains

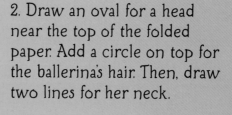

1. Fold a long rectangle of thin paper in half, so that the shorter edges meet. Then, fold the paper in half again. Crease the folds well.

2. Draw an oval for a head near the top of the folded paper. Add a circle on top for the ballerina's hair. Then, draw two lines for her neck.

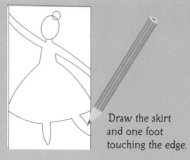

Draw the skirt and one foot touching the edge.

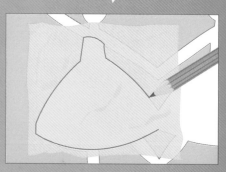

3. Draw the ballerina's arms at different angles, making them touch the edge on each side of the paper. Draw her body, skirt and feet.

4. Keeping the paper folded, cut out the ballerina. Don't cut along the folds at her hands, her skirt or one foot. Then, unfold the paperchain.

5. Lay a piece of tissue paper over one of the ballerinas. Trace along the sides of her body and skirt. Then, draw a curve at the top and bottom.

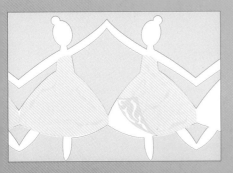

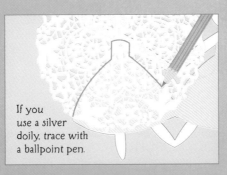

If you use a silver doily, trace with a ballpoint pen.

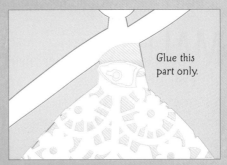

Glue this part only.

6. Cut out the tissue paper dress and glue it on. Then, trace tissue paper dresses for the other ballerinas and glue them on, too.

7. Lay a paper doily on top of a ballerina so that the edge of the doily lies along the bottom of the skirt. Trace around her dress and cut out the shape.

8. Glue the top part of the doily and press it onto the her dress. Then, trace and cut out dresses for the other ballerinas and glue them on.

These two ballerinas had smaller pieces of doilies glued onto their dresses.

Draw the spiral at the top of the hair.

9. Draw around the faces with a silver pen. Draw the hair and add rows of dots for straps. Add eyes, too. Draw the lips with a pink pencil.

You could cut little strips from a silver doily and glue them on, too.

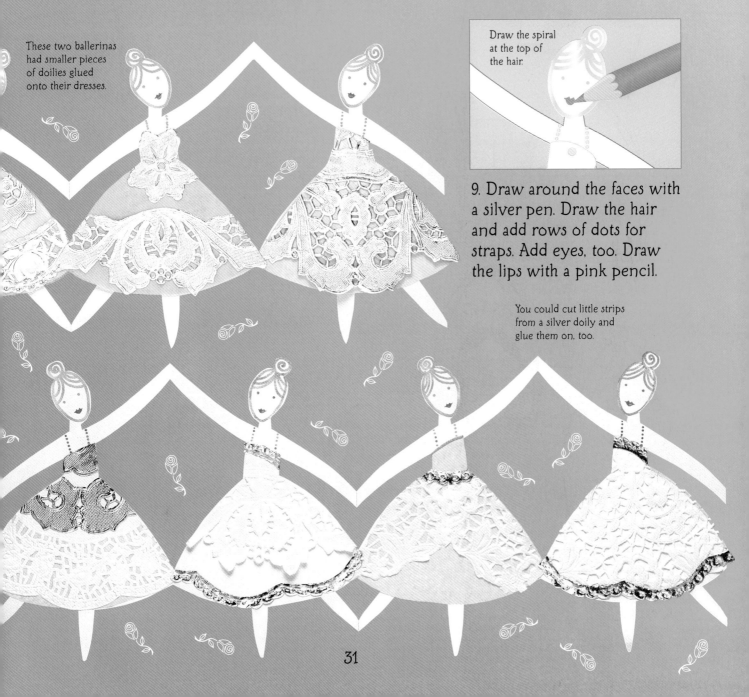

Hairstyles, crowns and tiaras

7.2.14

MALPAS

This page shows you lots more ideas for drawing different hairstyles, crowns and tiaras on your princesses and ballerinas. You could use these ideas for the princesses in the windows on pages 6-7, too.

Draw a curved crown, then add the veil hanging down on either side.

Draw patterns on a pointed headdress, then add wavy ribbons from the top.

Draw a little crown, then add a wavy bun on top.

Draw a band of fur with black dots and add a crown with jewels.

For an elegant hairstyle, draw the princess' hair piled high on her head, like the style below.

A ballerina usually wears a dainty crown, like this one, perched on top of her head.

Fill two curved shapes at each side of the head with crisscrossed lines.

For a tiara, draw a curve, then add overlapping loops and diamonds on top.

Draw crisscrossed lines on a ballerina's bun, to suggest a hairnet.

Draw lots of curly lines for ringlets, like the style above.

Draw lots of spirals, joined together, for a pretty ballerina headdress.

The princess below had two wavy lines drawn around her neck as a fancy collar.

Draw small crowns for a ballerina or a little princess.

Try a triangular tiara and add a jewel on a princess' forehead.

Photographic manipulation by John Russell, Nick Wakeford & Antonia Miller
This edition first published in 2013 by Usborne Publishing Ltd., 83-85 Saffron Hill, London, EC1N 8RT, England www.usborne.com